REACHING FOR SINAI

A Practical Handbook for Bar/Bat Mitzvah and Family

BY
RABBI RONALD H. ISAACS

RATNER MEDIA AND TECHNOLOGY CENTER
JEWISH EDUCATION CENTER OF CLEVELAND

RMC
246.2
KTAV Pub ISA
Hobo
14671

Isaacs, Ronald H.
Reaching for Sinai : A
practical handbook for
Bar/Bat Mitzvah and famil

Copyright © 1999
Ronald H. Isaacs

Manufactured in the United States of America

ISBN 0-88125-601-3

TABLE OF CONTENTS

Preface / 5
Some Historical Background / 7
The Bar and Bat Mitzvah Ceremony / 11
The Bar and Bat Mitzvah Service / 13
Being Commanded / 20
The Reception: Sanctifying the Celebration / 26
Life after Bar/Bat Mitzvah: Looking Ahead / 28

Appendix / 30
1. Sample Synagogue Brochure / 30
2. Sample Bar/Bat Mitzvah Synagogue Informational Booklet / 35
3. Bar/Bat Mitzvah Checklist / 38
4. Sample Letter / 40
5. Aliyot Blessings / 41
6. Sample Parent Speech / 42
7. Places for your Tzedakah / 44
8. Resources for Parents / 45
9. Torah and Haftarah Summaries / 46

Glossary / 62

Preface

The phone rings and an excited voice announces, "I cannot believe that I just received the date for my child's Bar/Bat Mitzvah. It only seems like yesterday that he/she began religious school." Such calls are filled with excitement and anticipation of an event that is laden with emotion and joy.

Although Bar and Bat Mitzvah ceremonies are common weekly occurrences, no two are exactly alike. Each one takes on special nuances of the particular family and of the congregation in which the ceremony takes place. The event is likely to remain one of the family's most treasured memories, leaving behind a host of special moments and personal mementos.

There are many decisions that need to be made, such as whom to invite, the persons to be honored during the service, the nature of the invitation, the kind of party, and so forth. All of these, and many more, can make the Bar or Bat Mitzvah a truly beautiful spiritual experience and not simply an elaborate birthday party. However, many Bar and Bat Mitzvah families lack the requisite knowledge and Judaic background to make the necessary informed decisions.

The purpose of this volume is to help families prepare for this important religious milestone. It is hoped that the book will anticipate many of your questions, help relieve your anxieties and guide you in making knowledgeable choices as you plan the details. Perhaps even more important, it will show the way to restoring a sense of spirituality to both the religious event itself and the celebration following.

The choices that you make as a family are crucial to shaping the event into the beautiful and inspiring experience that you no doubt would like it to be. It is my fondest wish that this book will guide you in reaching the path to that summit.

Congratulations and mazal tov!

Rabbi Ron Isaacs

Some Historical Background

At thirteen one is ready to fulfill commandments.
Ethics of Our Fathers 5:21

What is the meaning of the term Bar/Bat Mitzvah

The Aramaic word *bar* and the Hebrew word *bat* mean, respectively, "son" and "daughter." Thus, Bar Mitzvah means "son of the commandment," and Bat Mitzvah means "daughter of the commandment."

What event does Bar and Bat Mitzvah mark in Jewish life?

Becoming a Bar or Bat Mitzvah means that one has come of age under Jewish law and therefore is responsible for performing the mitzvot (religious commandments). The individual is no longer considered a minor or child, but rather is an adult with all the associated religious responsibilities and privileges associated with it. For boys, this event occurs at age thirteen; for girls at age twelve. In both cases, the age of majority is calculated in accordance with the birthday on the Jewish calendar.

What is the origin of the Bar Mitzvah ceremony.

The origin of the Bar Mitzvah ceremony is shrouded in mystery and debate. The Bible makes no mention of a Bar or Bat Mitzvah ceremony or of children becoming adults at age twelve or thirteen. In fact, the age mentioned in the Bible as a requirement or test for total participation in the activities of the Israelite community is twenty, not thirteen. Exodus 30:14 specifies that the census taken among the Israelites counted only those twenty and older. In Leviticus 27:1-5 the valuation of individuals for the redemption of vows to God is determined by age; persons between five and twenty are grouped together in valuation, which probably means that maturity came at twenty.

The Talmud, the major source for the rabbinic interpretation of Jewish law, is also silent with regard to a Bar Mitzvah at the age of thirteen, clearly indicating that the ceremony as we know it today was unknown in talmudic times. The Talmud does mention the term "Bar Mitzvah" twice, but both times in reference to any Jew who observes the religious commandments, not necessarily to a boy of thirteen. When referring to a boy of thirteen, the Talmud uses the term *bar onshin* ("one who is punishable"), indicating that in talmudic times a boy became liable at thirteen for any wrongdoing he might commit.

The clearest recognition of thirteen as the age when a child was considered to be a fully responsible member of the community is in the statement in the Mishnah, the earlier portion of the Talmud, that "at age thirteen one becomes subject to commandments" (Ethics of our Fathers 5:21).

There is a wide array of opinions on the reason why the thirteenth year was chosen as the age of performing mitzvot. Some ascribe it to foreign influences in Israel in the first century B.C.E. Others feel that it may be a throwback to ancient puberty rites of the sort practiced by many different peoples, for almost every culture in the world has an initiation rite of some kind to mark a child's entrance into puberty.

When did the "modern" Bar Mitzvah ceremony begin?

One of the first scholars to use the term *bar mitzvah* in the sense in which it is used today was Mordecai ben Hillel, a thirteenth century German rabbi. Most of the references to the *bar mitzvah* appear after this date.

It was on the Sabbath after the boy's thirteenth birthday that the Bar Mitzvah took place. The child was called to the Torah for the first time in his life, often for the *maftir aliyah* (This is the honor of chanting the concluding verses of the Torah portion and then the appropriate portion from the Prophets, called a Haftarah.) When the child finished his *aliyah,* the father would rise and say, "Blessed is God, Who has freed me from the responsibility for this boy." The text of this blessing, found in a *midrash* or homiletical interpretation of the Bible

(Genesis Rabbah 63:10), symbolizes that from that day on the parent is no longer responsible for the child's misdeeds and the child now has total responsibility for his own actions. This was followed by a meal of celebration (called a *seudat mitzvah*) at which the Bar Mitzvah would often deliver a Bible-related talk (called *devar Torah* in Hebrew) to show what he had learned.

Although it is likely that the Bar Mitzvah ceremony has gone through many changes since it first emerged in Jewish religious life, the basic idea remains. The ceremony is not a public display of a boy's vocal powers; rather, it is the occasion on which he enters fully into the religious heritage of the Jewish people. To signal this new status, he is given the privilege of leading the congregation in prayer, reciting a passage from the Prophets and the Torah, and being counted as one of the minyan.

What is the origin of the Bat Mitzvah ceremony?

Beginning in the second or the third century C.E. Jewish girls at age twelve took on legal responsibility for the performance of *mitzvot*. As with thirteen for boys, twelve probably corresponded to the age of the onset of puberty. Girls, however, were subject to fewer religious commandments than boys. They were exempted from a whole series of time-related positive commandments on the assumption that their domestic duties at home took precedence.

Many centuries passed before the Bat Mitzvah ceremony as we know it appeared. The first modern Bat Mitzvah was that of Judith Kaplan Eisenstein, whose father was Rabbi Mordecai Kaplan, the founder of the Reconstructionist movement. The Bat Mitzvah was held more than seventy years ago at a Shabbat service, where Judith recited the blessings, read a section from the Bible along with English translation, and concluded with the final blessings. Over the years the Bat Mitzvah ceremony was adopted by Conservative, Reform and Reconstructionist synagogues. Today it is usually held on Saturday morning, although in more traditional Conservative synagogues it is held on Friday evening and in some synagogues, Shabbat afternoon at Mincha (the afternoon service).

What is an Adult Bar or Bat Mitzvah?

It is never too late to celebrate a Bar or Bat Mitzvah. Many congregations today sponsor Bar and Bat Mitzvah classes as part of their adult studies programs. The classes generally include a commitment of a year or more of adult Jewish studies, culminating in a group Bar and Bat Mitzvah experience in which members of the class lead the service and chant a Haftarah.

In some congregations men and women who reach the age of eighty-three are afforded the opportunity to celebrate another Bar or Bat Mitzvah. This occasion, marking the passage of seventy years (regarded as the normal span of human life in the Bible), provides a wonderful opportunity for family, relatives and friends to celebrate an important milestone for a second time. When Judith Kaplan Eisenstein, America's first Bat Mitzvah celebrated her eighty-third birthday, she had a second Bat Mitzvah which was held on Shabbat afternoon!

The Bar/Bat Mitzvah Ceremony

From out of Zion comes the Torah.

Isaiah 2:3

When are Bar and Bat Mitzvah ceremonies held?

In most Conservative congregations today, Bar Mitzvah ceremonies may be held on any day that the Torah is read as part of the synagogue service: Monday, Thursday, Saturday, and Jewish holidays, including Rosh Hodesh (the celebration of a new Jewish month). Most Conservative congregations also permit Bat Mitzvah ceremonies on all days that the Torah is read. Others limit Bat Mitzvah ceremonies to the Friday evening Shabbat service.

How far in advance should a child begin to prepare for a Bar or Bat Mitzvah?

Most Conservative congregations require the successful completion of five years of formal religious study in addition to one year of specialized Bar/Bat Mitzvah training. Regular attendance at services is of paramount importance, since it affords an excellent opportunity to become familiar with the prayers, melodies, customs and rituals.

Who participates in the religious ceremony?

In addition to the Bar or Bat Mitzvah, it is customary for siblings, relatives and friends of the family to participate in the service. Many rabbis meet with the family of a Bar or Bat Mitzvah several months before the ceremony. At this meeting the rabbi will typically discuss the meaning of *mitzvot* (religious commandments) as they relate to becoming a Bar or Bat Mitzvah, the importance of continuing Jewish education, the meaning and theme of the Torah reading and Haftarah and the various parts of the service in which relatives and friends may participate (see Appendix 3 for a full list). In congregations that invite the parents of a Bar or Bat Mitzvah to address their child at the service, the rabbi may also discuss the nature of such an address and the kinds of things to include.

Are Bar and Bat Mitzvah ceremonies always celebrated in the synagogue?

Although most Bar and Bat Mitzvah ceremonies take place in the synagogue, some families prefer to celebrate the occasion in Israel. In such instances, the ceremony is typically held in Israeli Conservative, Reform or Reconstructionist synagogues, at the Western Wall in Jerusalem, or in the ancient synagogue at the top of Masada. Families that celebrate a Bar or Bat Mitzvah in Israel often opt for an additional celebration in their home synagogue. In this way friends and relatives who were unable to travel to Israel can be a part of the festivities.

The Bar/Bat Mitzvah Service

Praised are You, Adonai, Who gives us the Torah.
Siddur

What is the historical background of the Torah reading?

The Torah reading is the high point of the Bar and Bat Mitzvah ceremony. Exodus 24:7 describes how Moses took The Book of the Covenant and read it to the people. In Deuteronomy 31:12 the Israelites are enjoined to assemble at regular intervals to hear the words of the Torah. The Talmud (Bava Kamma 82a) relates that it was Ezra the Scribe who first introduced the practice of reading the Torah on Monday and Thursday mornings. Monday and Thursday were the market days when the farmers went to town to do their shopping and trading, and thus were able to attend to the service.

Although there have been periods when the tradition of publicly reading the Torah was neglected, it has been continuously observed in Jewish communities everywhere since the second century C.E. With the evolution of congregational worship, it was only natural that the Torah reading became an integral part of the service.

What are the components of the service for taking out the Torah?

The Torah is read publicly on Sabbaths, Mondays and Thursdays, and all Jewish festivals. The Torah service begins with the removal of the Torah scroll from the Ark. The congregation rises while the Ark is open. After the scroll is removed from the Ark, it is carried around the synagogue in a procession during which worshippers reach out to kiss it. The honors of opening and closing of the Ark are called the *petichot*. As the Torah scroll is read, there are several *aliyot* (different people going up to the bimah and chanting blessings before and after a section of the Torah is read aloud.) After the reading comes the lifting (*hagbah*) and tying (*gelilah*) of the Torah. Next the Haftarah (prophetic portion) is chanted. Finally, the Torah scroll is returned to the Ark after another procession around the synagogue. The number of aliyot and the number of Torah scrolls used at any given service vary according to the service and the time of year. On a typical Sabbath there are eight aliyot, including the last, which is called *maftir*. The *maftir* aliyah is given to the Bar or Bat Mitzvah of the day. On Mondays and Thursdays there are three aliyot, on Rosh Hodesh there are four, and on festivals there are five.

What is an aliyah?

The world *aliyah* is Hebrew for "to go up" or "to ascend." In a synagogue service it refers to going up to the bimah and reciting the blessings that precede and follow the Torah reading. The first Torah blessing emphasizes that God chose Israel to receive the Torah. After the first blessing has been recited, a section of the Torah is read which praises God for planting eternal life within us (see Appendix 5). This reading is followed by the second blessing. The last aliyah in a Sabbath or festival service is called the *maftir*, or concluding aliyah. It is reserved for the Bar or Bat Mitzvah, who in many instances will not only chant the two blessings but read from the Torah.

In most congregations aliyah honors are reserved for the family of the Bar or Bat Mitzvah, which is free to assign them as it wishes. Since it is customary to call up each person who has an aliyah by his or her Hebrew name, it is important to obtain the Hebrew names of your honorees in advance (see Appendix 4).

What are the *hagbah* and *gelilah* honors?

Following a custom that goes back to approximately the seventh century C.E., an honoree called the *hagbah* lifts the open Torah scroll in order to display the written text to the view of the entire congregation. The idea behind this ritual is that everyone in the congregation is given an opportunity to see the Torah and is able to proclaim:

וְזֹאת הַתּוֹרָה אֲשֶׁר שָׂם מֹשֶׁה לִפְנֵי בְּנֵי יִשְׂרָאֵל עַל פִּי יהוה בְּיַד מֹשֶׁה.

"This is the Torah that Moses placed before the children of Israel, the Torah given by God through Moses."

The person who lifts the Torah sits, while still holding the Torah, and another person, known as the *gelilah*, rolls the two ends of the scroll together, places a belt around the scroll to hold it in place, and "dresses" the Torah by placing the cover or mantle over it.

What is the Haftarah and the meaning of the blessings that are recited before and after it?

The word *haftarah* means "conclusion." Today it refers to the selection from one of the prophetic or historical books of the Bible that is chanted at the conclusion of the Torah reading. This tradition began in Palestine in the second century B.C.E., when the Syrians had forbidden the Jews to read the Torah (the first five books of the Bible). Selections from other biblical books were substituted; each was linked thematically to the weekly Torah portion. Over time, the reading of the Haftarah became a regular part of Sabbath and festival services.

Youngsters celebrating their Bar or Bat Mitzvah will typically chant a Haftarah if the service is held on the Sabbath or a festival. In addition to chanting the Haftarah, they also chant the five blessings preceding the Haftarah reading and the other four following it.

The blessing before the Haftarah expresses praise for the Israelite prophets and the authenticity of their message.

The first blessing after the Haftarah emphasizes God's faithfulness. The second blessing is a prayer for the return of the Jewish people to Jerusalem. The third blessing is a prayer for the coming of the Messiah, and the last blessing is a thank you to God for having given us the Torah, the prophets and the Holy Shabbat.

What are the *trop* or *ta'amei hamikra*?

Synagogue music has roots that go back to the time of the Temple in Jerusalem. In those days it was customary to chant the scriptual reading. The cantillation was governed by a series of musical notations called *trop* or *ta'amei hamikra*, which are found in the printed text of the Hebrew Bible either below or above each Hebrew word. These are the notes that each Bar or Bat Mitzvah learns in order to chant the Haftarah. The *trop* melodies for the Torah readings differ somewhat from those for the Haftarah, but they share the same basic inflections. The musical notes help to bring the words of the Torah and Haftarah to life, adding much drama to the recitation.

Which Torah portion or Haftarah will my child read?

There are two systems for dividing the Torah into weekly readings. In one, which originated in ancient Babylonia, the Torah is divided into fifty-four portions and read through in one year; in the other, which originated in Palestine, the Torah is read through in a three-year cycle. Every synagogue follows one or the other of these two systems; both specify the Torah portion to be read on every Sabbath of the year. Since every Torah portion has a specifically designated Haftarah associated with it, the Haftarah is also determined by the Torah-reading cycle. Your child's portion will be the one designated for the Sabbath on which the Bar or Bat Mitzvah takes place, a date usually determined by your child's birthday on the Hebrew calendar.

What can I expect my child to do in the service?

On a Sabbath or a festival it is customary for the Bar or Bat Mitzvah to have an aliyah, chant the Haftarah, and explain the meaning of the Torah/and or Haftarah portion to the congregation. Many Bar and Bat Mitzvah youngsters also read some of the Torah portion as well, depending upon their capabilities. Most synagogues also encourage them to lead parts of the service.

What honors are available to us and to whom should they be given?

Most rabbis meet with every Bar or Bat Mitzvah family several months in advance of the ceremony to discuss the service and its meaning. At that meeting the rabbi will review all the honors that are available. These generally include presenting the tallit to the Bar or Bat Mitzvah, opening and closing the Ark, being given aliyot, carrying the Torah scroll and lifting and "dressing" the Torah (see Appendix 3 for a list of honors).

It is important to bear in mind that other families in the congregation may have joyous events of their own to commemorate on the Sabbath of your Bar or Bat Mitzvah, and for this reason the rabbi may occasionally add honorees who are not related to you. For example, it is customary for the parents of a newborn infant to share an aliyah on the Sabbath when the child is named, a day that may coincide with your Bar or Bat Mitzvah. Similarly, it is customary for a groom-to-be, and sometimes the bride as well, to have an aliyah as part of the *Aufruf* ceremony on the Sabbath preceding the wedding.

In the spirit of sharing, families ought to reach out to each other on such occasions, so that the happiness of each *simchah* (joyous event) is compounded by the joy of the other celebration. For this reason it is customary for the family holding a naming ceremony or an *Aufruf* to share in the costs of the refreshments following services by co-sponsoring the Kiddush.

What can non-Jews do in the service?

The extent of a non-Jewish relative's participation will vary from synagogue to synagogue. Most congregations do not permit a non-Jew to say the blessings over the Torah. Many also do not permit non-Jews to participate in any of the other honors during the Torah service. Some permit a non-Jewish person to lead the congregation in a responsive supplementary reading. Consult your rabbi regarding the congregational policy.

What are some guidelines for parents who choose to address their child on his or her Bar/Bat Mitzvah?

Many Bar/Bat Mitzvah parents have adopted a practice based on the lovely old Jewish custom, established centuries ago, of writing an ethical will. In this document, normally prepared toward the end of life, parents would write a letter to their children in which they would sum up what they had learned over the years and express their hopes for the future. The scene in Genesis where Jacob gathers his children around his bed and tells them how to guide their lives after his death is usually regarded as a biblical model for the medieval ethical will. The example of the ethical will is a good one to keep in mind when preparing to address your children on the day of their Bar or Bat Mitzvah.

Many congregations invite the parents to join their child on the bimah and recited the *Shehecheyanu* prayer for the gift of life. This may be an appropriate time for you to address your child (see Appendix 6 for a sample speech). This is a sacred opportunity to share some thoughts on the meaning of the day. Here are several guidelines that you may wish to consider when preparing your own personal remarks:

1. Keep your remarks brief. Several minutes should be adequate to ensure that your message is clearly stated.

2. Do not say anything that might embarrass your child.

3. Include some of your hopes for your child's Jewish future now that he or she has become the newest Jewish man or woman.

4. Try to include some statements about important family values that you hope your child will continue to embrace and transmit.

5. Try to include a quotation from a Jewish source or apply a teaching from the weekly Torah portion.

6. Speak from the heart and be personal.

What are some guidelines for personalizing the worship service?

Many Bar and Bat Mitzvah families have developed creative ways to personalize the service. Some congregations provide a Bar/Bat Mitzvah booklet that explains the service and includes the specific customs and rituals of the congregation (see Appendix 1). This is especially useful for less knowledgeable congregants and non-Jewish guests. Some congregations encourage families to create their own booklets for the service. (see Appendix 2). Such booklets typically include an explanation of the synagogue structure (e.g., Eternal Light, Holy Ark, etc.), the meaning of the tallit (prayer shawl), a brief explanation of the kipah (skullcap), and a listing of the honorees and their role in the service. The booklet might also include a list of *tzedakah* organizations to which guests may wish to consider contributing in honor of the Bar or Bat Mitzvah. Some families include an original English reading, prayer, or poem to enhance the service. Others choose to involve friends and family in leading various parts of the service, a practice that can offer warmth and a nice personal touch.

Some congregations have adopted the wonderful custom of inviting grandparents and parents to be on the bimah when the Torah is taken out of the Ark. After the scroll is removed, it is passed from the grandparents to the parents and then on to the Bar or Bat Mitzvah. The meaning, as the rabbi generally explains, is that the passing of the Torah through the generations of the family symbolizes the way in which it has been passed down through the generations of the Jewish people.

In some congregations, following an old custom, the worshippers throw candies at the Bar or Bat Mitzvah after the Haftarah reading is concluded. This symbolizes the wish for a sweet and joyous life, and is a lovely, fun-filled custom to follow. It is a good idea to choose very soft candies and to make sure they are wrapped. After the candies are thrown, the song *siman tov u-mazal tov* is often sung, accompanied by spontaneous hand clapping.

Being Commanded

We will hear and we will obey
Exodus 24:7

What is a mitzvah and how many are there in Judaism?

A mitzvah is a religious commandment. Although the word *mitzvah* is today often used to mean "good deed," it actually refers to a religious obligation or duty taught by the Torah and by rabbinic law. According to the traditional count, there are 613 commandments in the Torah; 248 of them are affirmative ("You shall do"), and 365 are negative ("You shall not do").

The most significant enumeration of the commandments is in the *Sefer Ha-Mitzvot*, written by the philosopher Maimonides around 1170 C.E. In it Maimonides cites the biblical source of all the mitzvot and discusses certain aspects of their observance. Indeed mitzvot are at the very core of Judaism. Their observance has preserved the vitality and traditions of the Jewish people from generation to generation.

What is the connection between mitzvot and becoming a Bar or Bat Mitzvah?

Becoming a Bar or Bat Mitzvah means becoming subject to the commandments and being responsible for carrying them out. A youngster who becomes a Bar or Bat Mitzvah ought to take on ways of living and thinking and seeing the world from the perspective of God. The age of mitzvot is a time of choice. Every Bar and Bat Mitzvah has the serious duty of choosing to be commanded and accepting new responsibilities as a Jew.

What is the significance of the mitzvah of wearing a tallit?

In many Conservative synagogues (and in some Reform and Reconstructionist too), it is customary for boys (and often girls who so wish) to wear a tallit for the first time on the occasion of their Bar or Bat Mitzvah. In some congregations a family member is called to the bimah to present the tallit to the child.

The tallit, or prayer shawl, is a four-cornered garment which has *tzitzit*, or fringes, attached to each corner. The fringes are reminders of God's commandments, in keeping with Numbers 15:37-41, which states that every time we look at the fringes we are to remember God's commandments. Wearing a tallit is obligatory for all Jewish adult males. It is an optional commandment for Jewish women, since women were given a rabbinic exemption from positive time-related commandments, such as wearing the tallit, on the assumption that their domestic duties in the home took precedence.

What is the mitzvah of wearing tefillin, and why are they worn by adult Jewish males (and some adult Jewish females) at weekday morning services?

Tefillin, or phylacteries, are leather boxes containing strips of parchment with straps attached. Both the tefillin of the head (called the *tefillin shel rosh*), and the tefillin of the arm (called the *tefillin shel yad*) contain parchments on which are written four biblical passages: Exodus 13:1-10, Exodus 13:11-16, Deuteronomy 6:4-9, and Deuteronomy 11:13-21. The tefillin of the arm consists of a single compartment, containing these four passages in four parallel columns on a single piece of parchment. The tefillin of the head has four separate compartments, one for each passage. The passages stress the duty of loving and serving God by following God's commandments. Since we are to subject our thoughts and actions to the service of God, we wear tefillin on the head, symbolizing our mental faculties, and on the left arm next to the heart, symbolizing the seat of our emotions.

The tefillin are worn by adult males (and adult females who choose to do so) at weekday morning services in conformity with the biblical command to "bind them for a sign upon your hand and for frontlets between your eyes" (Deuteronomy 6:8). Tefillin are not worn on Sabbaths or festivals, because they were intended to serve as a symbol of the covenant between God and the Jewish people, and since the Sabbath and the festivals are also symbols of the covenant, wearing tefillin would be superfluous.

What are some other important mitzvot for every Bar and Bat Mitzvah to consider?

Many congregational schools require Bar and Bat Mitzvah students to complete a mitzvah project. This project is intended to make students research and begin to experience a whole series of different mitzvot, thereby becoming familiar with the range of possibilities. The following is a list of mitzvot in various categories along with several related projects, taken from a cross section of religious schools:

Learning

1. Find a biblical verse or a quotation from a Jewish source. Write it down, giving its origin. Explain it in your own words and illustrate it either with your own illustration or with pictures cut out of a magazine or newspaper.

2. Read a book on a Jewish theme and write a book report summarizing its main points. Explain how this book relates to Judaism and tell what you have learned about Jews or Judaism from it. Would you recommend this book to others?

3. Create a Jewish Family Scrapbook that includes your family tree.

4. List seven places in Israel you would like to visit and explain why you want to visit them. Pinpoint the places on a map of Israel.

5. Visit a Jewish museum with your family and write a report on

your feelings and reactions to the exhibits and what you learned from the experience.

6. Present a discussion/program for your class or write a paper describing the attitudes and concerns of members of your family about Jewish life in America today.

7. Establish a family pen-pal relationship with a Jewish family on the Conservative Kibbutz Hanaton. Prepare a scrapbook of letters sent and received and a summary of insights gained by each participating family member.

8. Design a family crest which communicates your family's Jewish values and history.

9. Label one window in your home to be the *Mah rabu ma'asecha Adonai* ("How manifold are your works, O God") viewing station. Keep a written or pictorial record of aspects of creation seen during a daily check.

Prayer

1. Attend two festival services. (e.g., Passover, Shavuot, Rosh Hodesh) or two weekday services. Write a report on how they differ from a Shabbat service.

2. Lead your family in the Friday evening Shabbat rituals for one month at home.

3. Learn the Havdalah service and lead it for a minimum of three months.

Holiday Celebration

1. Fast for a full day on one of the Jewish fast days. Explain the meaning of the fast day you selected.

2. Write an original holiday song (including words and melody).

3. Do a Passover project in music, photography, or art related to the meaning of freedom.

4. Design a poster showing the origins of Thanksgiving in the United States and of Sukkot in biblical Judaism. Show the similarities and differences.

5. Read a story about Hanukkah that explains why we light eight candles. Write a story or play about eight modern reasons for lighting the candles at Hanukkah time.

Tzedakah

1. Make a family *tzedakah* box and contribute to it each week.

2. Research Maimonides' Eight-Step Ladder of Charity. Explain in you own words how Maimonides understands charity in its various forms.

3. Make a list of the Jewish agencies in your area that collect *tzedakah*. Tell how the funds are used.

4. Choose a *tzedakah* hero and research this person. What is his or her *tzedakah*? In your opinion, why is this person a hero?

Gemilut Hasadim: Deeds of Lovingkindness

1. Adopt an elderly person or a shut-in and contact this person on a regular basis.

2. Volunteer to help and/or work with a handicapped child or adult.

3. Get involved in the Mazon hunger organization.

4. Volunteer for your local U.S.A. Super Sunday.

5. Write to an elected official about a social or political issue that is important to you.

6. Participate with your family in a clothing drive for the needy.

7. Adopt a recently arrived Russian immigrant family.

8. Encourage your local bakeries and caterers to channel leftovers to a food bank.

9. Adopt the "*tzedakah* habit" of buying an extra item of food every time you go grocery shopping for distribution to the needy.

The Reception: Sanctifying the Celebration

*Eat your bread with gladness,
and drink your wine with a joyous heart.*

Ecclesiastes 9:7

What are the religious observances related to the Bar/Bat Mitzvah reception?

The festive meal and/or Kiddush that follows the Bar or Bat Mitzvah ceremony is an opportunity for family and friends to celebrate the joy of the occasion. Since the meal is a *seudat mitzvah* (religious meal), it ought to take on an aura of sanctity. Unfortunately, there has always been a tendency for families, both past and present, to make celebrations elaborate. Back in 1595 in Cracow, Poland, for instance, the rabbinic authorities levied a communal tax on Bar Mitzvah feasts so as to keep them within the bounds of good taste. Judaism has always urged people to use moderation to ensure that the spiritual significance of the event is not lost.

When planning the menu you will surely wish to make it a kosher one so that all of the guests, including observant ones, can enjoy the meal. Beginning the meal with the *Hamotzi* blessing over the bread and concluding it with the *Birkat Hamazon*, or Grace after Meals, are additional ways of bringing God into the party. Even the choice of music can affect the atmosphere. Spirited Israeli dancing and Jewish music will undoubtedly invest the party with deeper Jewish feeling.

What are some other creative ways of enhancing the Bar/Bat Mitzvah party?

Many families have created ways to invest the party with added sanctity. Here are some ideas for you to consider:

1. Instead of flowers as the centerpieces, use Jewish books standing upright as your table decorations. At the end of the party, the books can either be given to the guests or donated to the synagogue library.

2. Include with the placecard settings information about the Mazon hunger relief organization, and encourage your guests to contribute to it.

3. Arrange in advance to give the leftover food to a local food bank.

4. Have each guest come up to light a candle on the cake. Ask them in advance to be prepared to offer a blessing or mention a Jewish value when they do so.

5. Instead of giving souvenir party favors to the guests, plant trees in Israel in their honor and give out the tree certificates as mementos.

6. Ask guests to bring canned food, clothing or toys to the party for subsequent distribution to the homeless.

7. Give a percentage of the cost of your Bar or Bat Mitzvah celebration to Mazon, the Jewish Hunger Fund.

8. If you use flowers as centerpieces at the party, donate them to a hospital or a home for the aged.

9. Buy an Israel bond in honor of your guests and display it prominently at the party.

10. Display your family tree in a prominent place at the party.

Life after Bar Bat Mitzvah: Looking Ahead

Life is a partnership of God and man.

Abraham Joshua Heschel

What are some important tasks that lie ahead for a Bar or Bat Mitzvah?

Studying Torah, being involved in Judaism and the synagogue and actively pursuing the experience of doing mitzvot are sound goals for every Bar and Bat Mitzvah. In many synagogues, youngsters are encouraged to chant Haftarot and Torah readings for Shabbat, festivals and even the High Holy Days. Being involved in a synagogue youth group is an important way to stay in touch with Judaism. Continuing one's Jewish education can be of paramount importance for spiritual sustenance and moral nourishment; so is regular attendance at synagogue services. And of course, it is also important to add to one's personal repertoire of mitzvot observed. Through all these means, young people are able to continue the lifelong process of becoming authentic sons and daughters of the commandment.

What are some practical mitzvah suggestions for the future?

The following are several practical mitzvah suggestions that a Bar or Bat Mitzvah may wish to consider. Many of them are based on "116 Practical Mitzvah Suggestions" and "11 Ways U.S.Yers can Change the World in Big Ways," both by Danny Siegel.

1. Establish a committee at your synagogue to take leftover flowers from the sanctuary and from Jewish communal events to shelters, hospitals, and the like.

2. Open a separate checking account for *tzedakah* and make frequent deposits into it.

3. Contribute each year to the U.J.A. campaign, and try to serve as a volunteer for U.J.A. Super Sunday.

4. Contribute the money you would have used for food on Yom Kippur or other fast days to Mazon and other organizations to help feed the hungry.

5. Adopt the *"tzedakah* habit" of buying an extra item of food whenever you go grocery shopping for distribution to the hungry.

6. Establish a food pantry in your local synagogue.

7. When you are old enough, give blood.

8. Volunteer to help lead holiday celebrations in homes for the aged.

9. Adopt a recently arrived Russian family.

10. Consult the rabbi to see if you can help make a minyan for people in mourning who are sitting shiva.

11. Set up a mitzvah crib in the lobby of your synagogue. The crib will be the collection point for items for infants and young children whose families cannot afford to purchase them. Make an attractive sign listing the kinds of items you are looking for.

12. Plant a vegetable garden on the lawn of your synagogue and donate the food grown to a soup kitchen.

13. Since many shoe stores throw discontinued styles away, try to encourage them to donate these shoes to a local shelter or some agency that provides for the poor.

14. Buy a large-print siddur for use by the visually impaired.

Appendix

1. Sample Synagogue Brochure

At many Bar and Bat Mitzvah ceremonies, there is too little participation. Guests often arrive late. Some feel uncomfortable in a new synagogue where customs and prayer melodies are different from those to which they are accustomed. Non-Jewish guests may be attending a synagogue for the first time. Even some of the Jewish guests may be strangers to the synagogue and unfamiliar with Jewish worship services.

For all these reasons, it is very important for families that will be celebrating a Bar or Bat Mitzvah to become acquainted with the customs and ceremonies of the synagogue where the ceremony will take place. The more familiar you are with the melodies and words of the prayers, the more meaningful the service will be to you. The following is a brochure which is given to Bar and Bat Mitzvah guests in one synagogue to help them better understand and participate in Sabbath services. If you find this brochure helpful, feel free to use it as is, or to adapt it, for distribution to your own Bar or Bat Mitzvah guests.

SAMPLE BROCHURE

Welcome to our Sabbath Service

INTRODUCTION

This brochure is provided to help our guests better understand and participate in our Sabbath services. Additional introductory information can be found at the beginning of our prayerbook.

The Sabbath, the weekly anniversary of God's creation of the world, is a spiritual pause during which we can reevaluate our lives and the world in which we have our being. It is an occasion to regenerate our energies for the task of bringing the real world in line with the kind of world God intended when God created it. To accomplish these ends, Jewish practice sets aside part of the Sabbath day for prayer, meditation, and study of Torah.

Worship services at Temple Sholom are conducted by and for the congregation. Men and women participate equally. Young people are especially welcome. Conservative Judaism at Temple Sholom has no observers, only participants.

The rabbi leads the service, comments on the Torah or Haftarah, and delivers a sermon or leads a discussion based on the Bible reading of the day. The cantor leads the congregation in song and chants the Torah reading. The Bar/Bat Mitzvah leads part of the service and chants the Haftarah. You make this a holy gathering by sharing in our ritual.

While the order of the service has been fixed for many centuries, the content has been evolving for just as long. In the Jewish tradition, the liturgical door has always been open for new prayers or new versions of old prayers. You may hear some today. Your guide to these prayers is the *siddur* (prayerbook). The high point of the Shabbat service is the reading of the Torah. Please follow along in the *Chumash* (Bible), which is both in Hebrew and in English translation. We request that you restrict your movements and greetings during this time. We further request that you neither enter nor leave the sanctuary when the congregation is standing, when the Holy Ark is open, or when the rabbi is speaking.

At the conclusion of the service, please return all *siddurim* (prayerbooks), *Chumashim* (Bibles), and *tallitot* (prayer shawls) to the rear of the sanctuary. There the ushers will collect them.

All males are expected to keep their heads covered at all times. Of course, this being the Sabbath, there is no smoking or picture-taking in or on the temple property. As is our custom, the entire congregation, members and guests, are invited to partake of the Kiddush, the collation immediately following the service.

THE SHACHARIT SERVICE

Our Sabbath morning service begins with Passages of Song. This introductory section sets the mood and establishes the basis for prayer. It is an anthology of biblical selections, mainly from the Book of Psalms, which celebrates God's power as the Creator and our thankfulness and gratitude for God's providential care.

Shacharit (the official morning service) begins and the worshippers rise to respond to the *Barechu*, the call to congregational prayer. The hymn *El Adon*, which follows, pays homage to God for creating the heavenly bodies.

The congregation dramatically affirms its faith in God by chanting *Shema Yisrael*, "Hear, O Israel, Adonai is our God, Adonai is One!" This is followed by selections from two books of the Torah, Deuteronomy and Numbers, in which the Jew is bidden to love God, study and transmit our traditions to the children, observe the practices of Jewish life, and remember the spiritual goals for which our ancestors were redeemed from bondage.

The *Amidah* is the core of the worship service. It is a series of seven benedictions recited silently while standing and gives expression to our thanksgiving and special joy in the Sabbath.

Following the silent recitation of the *Amidah*, it is repeated publicly and the *Kedushah* (Prayer of Sanctification) is added. The *Kedushah* is a poem of mystic origin inspired by the famous vision of the prophet Isaiah: "holy, holy, holy is the God of Hosts, the whole universe is filled with God's glory." The Shacharit service concludes with the Kaddish prayer, in which God's Name is magnified.

THE TORAH SERVICE

Removing the Torah from the Ark

Study is an integral part of the Jewish experience. The Torah study segment of our service begins with the removal of the Torah scroll (s) from the Holy Ark. The congregation rises and then the Torah is taken in a joyous processional around the sanctuary, symbolizing that the knowledge of the Torah and its observances are incumbent on all Jews.

Torah Study

Chumash (Pentateuch)

After the scroll is placed on the reader's desk, the Torah reading and study begin, and the Pentateuch (Five Books of Moses) is used for this part of the service. Each page of this book contains Hebrew text and English translation side by side, with footnotes below referenced to the numbers of the respective verses.

The designated portion *(sedrah)* for each Sabbath morning is divided into seven or more parts (aliyot), all chanted in an ancient musical mode. For each portion an adult is called from the congregation and given the honor of reciting two blessing—one prior to the Torah reading and the other following.

At the conclusion of the Torah reading, the scroll is raised and shown to the congregation. The congregation rises and chants "This is the Torah which Moses placed before the people of Israel, by the word of God through the hand of Moses."

Lessons from the Prophets

In addition to the Pentateuch lesson, a related and significant selection from the Prophets, called the Haftarah, is chanted. This portion is chanted in a traditional tune different from that of the Torah portion. The opportunity to recite the blessings for the final Torah section *(maftir)* and to chant the prophetic portion is traditionally given to a Jewish youth who has just become a Bar or Bat Mitzvah. By this act the young person signifies to the congregation his or her readiness to accept the responsibilities and obligations incumbent upon an adult member of the Jewish people.

Return the Torah to the Ark

At the conclusion of the prophetic reading, we return to the prayerbook and recite Psalm 145.

The service for replacing the Torah includes the chanting of Psalm 29 as the scroll is again taken in processional and returned to the ark. As the Torah is replaced in the ark, a prayer is chanted by the congregation, and after the ark is closed, a brief form of the *Kaddish* doxology is recited to mark the end of the Torah section of the worship.

THE MUSAF SERVICE

An additional *Amidah* called *Musaf* is included on all special days, such as the Sabbath, Rosh Hodesh (the New Month), and festivals. The Musaf *Amidah* is said while standing, and it recalls our ancestors' celebration of the Sabbath while also giving expression to our joy in its observance. During the Musaf *Amidah*, another *Kedushah* poem is recited to proclaim the holiness of God.

Following the *Amidah*, the congregation sings *Ein Keilohenu*, proclaiming that God is unique and unlike any other.

The congregation now rises for the *Aleinu*. In this prayer we proclaim God as the Sovereign Ruler of the Universe.

Those who are within the first year of mourning for a close relative or who are marking an anniversary of a death join in reciting the Mourner's Kaddish. Transcending their grief, the mourners rise in the midst of the congregation to affirm faith in God's justice and sanctify God's Name. The rest of the congregation responds to the words of the mourners.

It is the practice at Temple Sholom for the family of every Bar and Bat Mitzvah to join their children on the bimah. They are given an opportunity to share their joy by saying some words to their child. This is followed by the recitation of the *Shehecheyanu* prayer, the prayer for the gift of life. At the conclusion of this prayer, several presenters are called to give the Bar or Bat Mitzvah a gift in honor of the presenter's affiliate organization within the temple.

The final prayer is *Adon Olam*, in which God is proclaimed as the Eternal One. Following this hymn, the congregation joins together at the Kiddush, a reception where the sanctity of the Sabbath is publicly declared over a cup of wine, symbol of joy. This is followed by *Hamotzi*, the blessing over the bread.

2. Sample Bar/Bat Mitzvah Synagogue Informational Booklet

(Feel free to adapt what follows to meet your specific situation and congregational practices)

Welcome to Adam's Bar Mitzvah. The Bar Mitzvah celebration as we know it today originated in the Middle Ages, and marks the coming of age with regard to religious responsibilities and imposed obligations. Children study for many years before they are called to the Torah to chant.

There may be some "strange" sights at Temple Sholom. This is an explanation of some of them.

When you first enter the sanctuary you will notice a box filled with *yarmulkes* or *kippot* in Hebrew. Wearing a head covering is a way of showing reverence to God.

Next, there is a rack of *tallitot* (prayer shawls). The *tallit* is worn on the Sabbath, mostly by men, although some women may choose to wear one as well. The *tallit* is a reminder to observe God's laws. Originally, the word meant "cloak" or "blanket." The cloak worn in ancient times probably looks very similar to the *abbaya* (blanket) still worn by the Bedouins as a protection against the weather.

On the four corners of the *tallit* hang the *tzitzit*, or fringes. The reason for wearing the fringes comes from the Book of Numbers 15:37-41: "Speak to the children of Israel and bid them to affix fringes to the corners of the garments...that they may look at them and remember all the commandments of God."

The ushers will give you a *siddur* (prayerbook) and a *Chumash* (Bible) upon entering the Sanctuary. The *siddur* is the smaller book and has Hebrew on the right-hand pages (even-numbered) and the English translation on the left-hand pages (odd numbered). The larger book, the *Chumash*, will be referred to during the Torah service. This book contains the words of the Torah as well as the Prophets. Please note that both books open " backwards," from left to right.

The rabbi sits on the right hand side of the *bimah* (the raised portion in front of the congregation). The cantor, who chants the liturgy, stands on the left hand side of the *bimah*.

The Holy Ark is in the center of the *bimah*. This is where the Torah scrolls are kept. It has two doors and a curtain inside. The designs on the door depict the symbols of the twelve tribes of Israel (Jacob's sons).

Above the Holy Ark is the *Ner Tamid*, or Eternal Light. This light is always kept burning. In Temple times there was a part of the *menorah* (candelabrum) in the Jerusalem Temple which was constantly fed with oil in order to burn continuously. This light, which was the western-most branch of the *Menorah* was called the *Ner Maaravi*, or Western Lamp. It was a source of light from which the other six lights, which were extinguished and cleaned daily, could be lit.

On the right side of the *bimah* stands our *menorah* (candelabrum). Like the *menorah* in the ancient Jerusalem Temple, its lights symbolize the eternal faith of the Jewish people.

THE SHABBAT SERVICE

The Shabbat morning is divided into three separate services- a preliminary service (the so-called "warm- up prayers"), the Shacharit Morning service, which includes the Torah service and the additional Musaf service. Among the important prayers in the Shacharit service are the *Barechu*, which is the congregational call to prayer, the *Shema Yisrael* which affirms our faith in One God, and the *Amidah*, a series of seven benedictions, recited silently while standing, which give expression to our thanksgiving and special joy in the Sabbath.

The study segment of the service begins with the removal of the Torah scroll(s) from the Holy Ark. The congregation rises and the Torah in taken in a joyous procession around the sanctuary, symbolizing that knowledge of Torah and its observance are incumbent on all Jews.

The designated reading for each Sabbath morning is divided into seven or more parts. For each portion an adult is called to the Torah for an *aliyah*, reciting two blessings. At the conclusion of the Torah reading the scroll is raised by the *magbeah* (the person who lifts the Torah scroll), also known as the *hagbah*, and shown to the congregation. The congregation rises and chants, "This is the Torah which Moses placed before the people of Israel, by the word of God through the hand of Moses." A second person. called the *gollel*, also known as the *gelilah*, rolls the Torah scroll together and replaces the mantle and its embellishments.

Following the reading of the Torah, the Bar Mitzvah Adam will chant the prophetic portion called the *Haftarah*. This practice started in the second century B.C.E. when the Jewish people were forbidden to study the Torah. Instead, they found passages from the Books of the Prophets that could be associated with the Torah portion of the week. Later, when Jews again could study the Torah without fearing for their lives, they continued with the custom of reading a *Haftarah*.

After the reading of the Haftarah, the Torah scroll is returned to the Ark. The additional Musaf service is now chanted. In this prayer we recall our ancestors' celebration of the Sabbath while also giving expression to our own joy in its observance.

The service concludes with the *Aleinu* prayer, in which God is proclaimed Ruler of the universe, then the Mourner's *Kaddish* and *Adon Olam*.

It is the practice at Temple Sholom (a Conservative egalitarian congregation) for the congregation to share in the simchah of the occasion by presenting gifts to the Bar/Bat Mitzvah, just before the rabbi's final comments.

Following the final hymn, *Adon Olam* (God the Eternal One), the congregation joins together at the *Kiddush*, a reception where the sanctity of the Sabbath is publicly declared over a cup of wine, symbol of joy.

RULES (the no-nos)

1. No taking of photographs.

2. No smoking.

3. No writing.

4. No giving or handling of money (i.e. no offering during services).

5. No eating before the blessing is said over the bread.

6. No phone calls.

PHRASES YOU MIGHT HEAR AT SERVICES

1. *Shabbat*: The Sabbath, the seventh day of the Jewish week.

2. *Shabbat Shalom*: Sabbath Peace, a greeting.

3. *Gut Shabbos*: "Have a good Sabbath."

4. *Mazal tov*: Congratulations.

5. *Simchah*: Joyous event.

6. *Challah*: Braided bread eaten on the Sabbath.

7. *Hamotzi*: Blessing over the bread.

8. *Shalom:* Peace, hello, goodbye.

3. Bar/Bat Mitzvah Checklist

This list will help keep you organized when planning your Bar/Bat Mitzvah.

Date of Bar/Bat Mitzvah _____

Name of Torah and Haftarah portion _____

I have sent out invitations.

Name of florist_____

Name of photographer _____

Name of caterer_____

We have selected the participants in the service and reminded those who will chant blessings to review them. They are:

Ark Openers and Closers

English Names _____

Hebrew Names _____

Aliyot:

1. English and Hebrew Names _____

2. English and Hebrew Names _____

3. English and Hebrew Names _____

4. English and Hebrew Names _____

5. English and Hebrew Names _____

6. English and Hebrew Names _____

7. English and Hebrew Names _____

8. (Maftir) English and Hebrew Names of Bar/Bat Mitzvah
_____

Lift Torah (*Hagbah*) English and Hebrew Names _____

Tie Torah (*Gelilah*) English and Hebrew Names _____

Other Parts in Service:
Name _____ Part _____

Name _____ Part _____

Name of *Kiddush* chanter_____

Name of person leading *Hamotzi* (blessing over bread)_____

Name of person leading *Birkat Hamazon*
(blessing after meal)_____

Tzedakah organizations for contributions: _____

List of *mitzvot* that Bar/Bat Mitzvah has chosen to do in first year:
_____
_____

4. Sample Letter

The following is a letter written by a girl who was soon to become a Bat Mitzvah. In it she invites her honorees to accept an aliyah to the Torah. You may wish to adapt this letter for your own use.

Dear (Name),

I would like you to share the joy of my Bat Mitzvah with me by having the honor of saying the Torah blessings.

The Torah Service usually starts by 10 o'clock. The Torah blessings are found in the prayerbook on pages 400-402. You will be the (number) aliyah called to the Torah and will follow after (person).

After you have completed your aliyah, either the cantor or one of the gabbais will show you where to stand and let you know when to leave the bimah.

Please let me know your Hebrew name as soon as possible, so that it can be used when you are called to the Torah.

I am enclosing a copy of the Torah blessings. If you have any questions, please call me.

Looking forward to seeing you soon!

                            Love,

5. Aliyot Blessings

The following are the blessings that are chanted when a person is called to the Torah for an *aliyah*. You may wish to send these to your honorees and ask them to practice them in advance.

THE PERSON CALLED TO THE TORAH:

בָּרְכוּ אֶת יהוה הַמְבֹרָךְ:

Barechu et Adonai ha-mevorach
Praise God, Source of blessing

CONGREGATION

בָּרוּךְ יהוה הַמְבֹרָךְ לְעוֹלָם וָעֶד:

Baruch Adonai hamevorach l'olam va-ed.
Praised be God, Source of blessing, throughout all time.

PERSON CALLED TO THE TORAH

(Repeat the response and continue:)

בָּרוּךְ יהוה הַמְבֹרָךְ לְעוֹלָם וָעֶד:

בָּרוּךְ אַתָּה יהוה, אֱלֹהֵינוּ מֶלֶךְ הָעוֹלָם, אֲשֶׁר בָּחַר־בָּנוּ מִכָּל־הָעַמִּים וְנָתַן־לָנוּ אֶת, בָּרוּךְ אַתָּה יהוה, נוֹתֵן הַתּוֹרָה:

Baruch atah Adonai elohenu melech ha-olam asher bachar banu mikol ha-amim venatan lanu et torato. Baruch atah Adonai notayn ha-torah.

Praised are You, Adonai our God, Sovereign of the Universe, who has chosen us from all peoples by giving us the Torah. Praised are You, God, who gives the Torah.

(When Torah portion is completed)

בָּרוּךְ אַתָּה יהוה, אֱלֹהֵינוּ מֶלֶךְ הָעוֹלָם, אֲשֶׁר נָתַן לָנוּ תּוֹרַת אֱמֶת, וְחַיֵּי עוֹלָם נָטַע בְּתוֹכֵנוּ. בָּרוּךְ אַתָּה יהוה, נוֹתֵן הַתּוֹרָה:

Baruch atah Adonai elohenu melech ha-olam asher natan lanu torat emet v'chaye olam natah betochaynu. Baruch atah Adonai notayn ha-Torah.

Praised are You, Adonai our God, Sovereign of the universe, who has given us the Torah of truth, planting within us eternal life. Praised are You, God, Who gives the Torah.

6. Sample Parent Speech

(Some congregations encourage a parent (s) to speak to their child at this occasion)

Eric,

Over the last few weeks I have spent a lot of time thinking about what I was going to say to you today. I wanted it to be short and to the point and yet to leave you with something that you would remember when you thought about this day in the future. In the last couple of days I've been a little nervous as I struggled with finding what it was I was going to say.

The two messages that I want to leave you with today are about love and growing up. As you know, today represents your passage into adulthood. Well, that may be so and I think you will need more and more to take on the added responsibilities of growing up. But don't worry. Your mother and I will still be there to help you through it all. You don't have to grow up in one fell swoop today. But you will be growing up and I think both your mom and I are looking forward to it. I've enjoyed it so far, and I think I will continue to enjoy it. As you have grown older, I have enjoyed my interactions with you all the more, and I look forward to sharing with you the many experiences that you will go through in the next few years. I know, and you should also know, that they will not always be good and fun experiences. But it is necessary for you to go through all of them in order to grow into adulthood. And remember that through all of them, your sisters, mother, and I will be with you to help you deal with them.

Secondly, Eric, I want to talk with you a little about love. You know how important love is to me. All your life I have told you many times every day that I love you. As a matter of fact, I think I have told you so many times that you know that if I say to you "You know what Eric?" you would answer "You love me!"

We once talked a few years ago about why I say I love you so much. You asked why I told you so many times. And I told you all sorts of reasons, but in the end I said, and I repeat today, the reason that I tell you that I love you is because whenever I look at you, that is the feeling that I have. So, I can't help myself but to say what is in my heart to you. It makes me feel good to say it and I think it makes you feel good to hear it!

Eric, I spent a lot of time looking through many books trying to find a parable or saying or something that had already been written that would say what I was trying to say to you today. And I really couldn't find what I wanted to. The only thing I found was a prayer by General Douglas MacArthur, a general in World War II. I really liked what he wrote and I want to read it to you.

"Build me a son, O God, who will be strong enough to know when he is weak, and brave enough to face himself when he is afraid, one who will be proud and unbending in honest defeat, and humble and gentle victory.

Build me a son whose wishes will not take the place of deeds; a son who will know You, and that to know himself is the foundation stone of knowledge.

Lead him, I pray, not in the path of ease and comfort, but under the stress and spur of difficulties and challenge. Here let him learn to stand up in the storm; here let him learn compassion for those who fail.

> Build me a son whose heart will be clear, whose goal will be high; a son who will master himself before he seeks to master other men; one who will reach into the future, yet never forget the past.
>
> And after all these things are his, add, I pray, enough of a sense of humor, so that he may always be serious yet never take himself too seriously. Give him humility, so that he may always remember the simplicity of true greatness, the open mind of true wisdom, and the meekness of true strength.
>
> Then, I, his father, will dare to whisper, "I have not lived in vain."

Eric, so far you are already much of what I would like you to be, and I feel good that you will continue to grow into more of what your mother and I want you to become. I read somewhere that a man who has a son has the world's richest treasure. This is a day when I know that this true. You were born on Hanukkah, Eric, and you will always be our greatest gift. We love you very much!

7. Places for Your Tzedakah

The following is a list of organizations that perform *mitzvot* of lovingkindness. Your child may choose to give some of his or her gift money to one or more of these organizations in honor of becoming a Bar or Bat Mitzvah. Some families choose to include a *tzedakah* organization or two on the Bar/Bat Mitzvah invitation, suggesting that guests may wish to make a donation in honor of the Bar/Bat Mitzvah.

Foodbanks

Long Island Cares, Inc., POB 1073, West Brentwood, N.Y. 11717.
Yad Ezra Kosher Food Pantry, 26641 Harding, Oak Park, MI. 48237.
Hebrew Union College, Brookdale Center, 1 West 4th Street, New York, New York. 10012.
Passover Fund, B'nai Brith Project Hope, c/o Len Elenowitz, 8801 Post Oak Road, Potomac, MD 20854.
Foodbanks in your community

Other Tzedakah Organizations

American Red Magen David for Israel, 888 Seventh Avenue, Suite 403, New York, New York. 10016.
American Jewish World Service, 15 West 26th Street, New York, New York. 10010.
Beged Kefet, c/o Les Bronstein, 80 Cranberry Street, #9G, Brooklyn, New York. 11201.
Bet Tzedek, c/o Michael Feuer or Ralph Gottlieb, 145 S. Fairfax Ave., #200, Los Angeles, CA. 90036
Braille Haggadot: Jewish Heritage for the Blind, POB 336, Brooklyn, New York. 11229.

City Harvest, 11 John St., #503, New York, New York. 10038
Giraffe Project: Ann Medlock, POB 759, Langley, WA. 98260
Jewish Braille Institute (JBI), 110 E. 20th Street, New York, New York. 10016
Life Line for the Old, 14 Shivtei Yisrael St., Jerusalem, Israel.
MAZON, 2940 Westwood Blvd., #7, Los Angeles, CA. 90064.
Metropolitan New York Council on Jewish Poverty, 9 Murray Street, 4th Floor East, New York, New York. 10007
National Association for the Jewish Poor, 1163 Manor Ave, Bronx, New York. 10472.
Trevor's Campaign for the Homeless, 137 E. Spring Ave., Ardmore, Pa. 19003.
Ziv Tzedakah Fund, 263 Congressional Lane, #708, Rockville, MD. 20852

8. Resources for Parents

The following books can be used to help enhance the Bar and Bat Mitzvah experience.

Bell, Roselyn, ed. *The Hadassah Magazine Parenting Book*. New York: The Free Press, 1989.

Gillman, Neil. *Sacred Fragments: Recovering Theology for the Modern Jew*. Philadelphia: Jewish Publication Society, 1990.

Glatzer, Shoshana. *Coming of Age as A Jew*. New York: Board of Jewish Education, 1989.

Isaacs, Ronald H. *Rites of Passage*. Hoboken: Ktav Publishers, 1992.

Sidrah Reflections: A Guide to Sidrot and Haftarot. Hoboken: Ktav Publishing House, Inc., 1997.

Kadden, Barbara and Bruce. *Teaching Mitzvot*. Denver: Alternatives in Religious Education, 1988.

Katsh, Abraham I. ed. *Bar Mitzvah*. New York: Shengold Publishers, 1976.

Klein, Isaac. *A Guide to Jewish Religious Practice*. New York: Ktav Publishing House, Inc., 1979.

Kurshan, Neil. *Raising Your Child to be a Mensch*. New York: MacMillan Publishing Company, 1987.

Kushner, Harold. *Who Needs God*. New York: Summit Books, 1989.
Marcus, Audrey Friedman. *A Family Education Unit on Bar and Bat Mitzvah*. Denver: Alternatives in Religious Education, 1977.
Olitzky, Kerry M. and Isaacs, Ronald H. *Rediscovering Judaism: Bar and Bat Mitzvah for Adults*. Hoboken New Jersey: Ktav Publishing House, Inc., 1997.
Sanberg, Martin I. *Tefillin: "and you shall bind them..."* New York: United Synagogue of Conservative Judaism, 1992.
Siegel, Danny. *Gym Shoes and Irises: Personalized Tzedakah* (Books 1 and 2). Spring Valley, New York: Town House Press, 1982, 1987.
_____. *Mitzvahs*. Pittsboro, N.C. Townhouse Press, 1990.
_____. "11 Ways U.S.Y.ers Can Change the World in Big Ways or: How to Put your Mitzvah Power Hungriness to Work". Tikkun Olam Program of United Synagogue Youth.

9. Torah and Haftarah Summaries

The Torah is also known as the Five Books of Moses and the Pentateuch. The first book of the Torah begins with the story of the creation of the world; the last book concludes the life of Moses. Each week a different *sedrah* (Torah portion) is read. On Sabbaths and most Jewish holidays the Torah reading is followed by the reading of the Haftarah, a selection from one of the historical or prophetic books of the Bible. Here is a list of the weekly and holiday Torah and Haftarah portions and a brief summary of their contents. You will notice that each Haftarah has a thematic link with the Torah portion to which it is connected. Once you identify the Torah portion and Haftarah for your son or daughter, you may wish to refer to this summary and discuss with your child the portion's meaning, significance, and implications. You may also wish to use it as a handy reference throughout the year.

Genesis

Contents: The world is created. The lives of the three patriarchs Abraham, Isaac, and Jacob are portrayed. At the end of the book Jacob and his sons go down to Egypt. Jacob blesses his sons before his death.

Weekly Portions

1. *Bereshit* (1:1-6:8): The world is created in six days.
Haftarah (Isaiah 42:5-43:10): A message of hope is given to the Israelites exiled in Babylon after the destruction of the first Temple. God will redeem them, but they must keep their faith strong and truly become a "light to the nations."

2. *Noah* (6:9-11-11:32): A major flood destroys the entire world; God's rainbow is the first covenantal "sign" that the world will never again be destroyed in its entirety.
Haftarah (Isaiah 54:1-55:5): The Babylonian exile is compared to the flood. Both were punishments for wrongdoing. The Israelites will again be redeemed because of God's eternal kindness and grace.

3. *Lech Lecha* (12:1-17:27): God tells Abraham to leave Mesopotamia for the Promised Land. God makes a covenant with Abraham, promising that he will be the father of the Jewish people. The eternal sign of this covenant is circumcision.
Haftarah (Isaiah 40:27-41:16): The exiled Israelites in Babylon are assured that redemption is forthcoming because of the covenant God made with Abraham.

4. *Vayera* (18:1-22:24): Abraham welcomes three angels into his tent and learns that his wife Sarah, will give birth to a son. Abraham pleads with God not to destroy the cities of Sodom and Gomorrah. Unable to find ten righteous people, Abraham accepts God's decision. The cities are destroyed; Lot's wife turns back to look at the cities and is transformed into a pillar of salt. Abraham is prepared to carry out God's will and sacrifice his son, but at the last moment, as Isaac is bound on the altar, the angel of God intervenes.
Haftarah (II Kings 4:1-37): The prophet Elisha provides a poor widow with oil so that she can pay off her creditors and then saves a child who has suffered a stroke.

5. *Chayyei Sarah* (23:1-25:18): Eliezer, the servant of Abraham, is sent to find a wife for Isaac. Rebekah offers his camels water to drink. Because of her kindness, she is chosen to be Isaac's wife.

Haftarah (I Kings 1:1-31): As King David's death approaches, his son Adonijah prepares to assume the throne. Bathsheba informs David of the plot, and he promises that Solomon will succeed him.

6. *Toledot* (25:19-28:9): Twins are born to Isaac and Rebekah. The younger Jacob, "steals" the birthright from the elder, Esau, then flees to Mesopotamia to avoid being killed by Esau.

Haftarah (Malachi 1-2:7): The last of the prophets criticizes the priests who are in charge of the Temple, reminding them that God wants more than sacrificial animals. God wants truth and kindness, the real purpose for which Jacob and his descendants were chosen over Esau.

7. *Vayetze* (28:10-32:3): God appears to Jacob in a dream. Jacob works fourteen years for Laban and was supposed to marry Rachel, but was tricked into marrying Leah as well. He hopes to reconcile with Esau, whom he has not seen in twenty years.

Haftarah (Hosea 12:13-14:10): Envisioning the destruction that lies ahead for the Northern Kingdom of Israel, Hosea alerts the Israelites to cease their wrongdoing. He tells them to return to God and repent before it is too late.

8. *Vayishlach* (32:4-36:43): Jacob and Esau meet after twenty years. The night before, Jacob has a fierce struggle with an unknown opponent. He emerges victorious and is blessed with a new name, Israel, meaning "He who strives with God." Rachel dies and is buried in Bethlehem.

Haftarah (Obadiah 1:1-21): Obadiah criticizes Edom, descendant of Esau and the enemy of Israel, for its treacherous behavior toward the Israelites.

9. *Vayeshev* (37:1-40:23): Jacob presents a coat of many colors to Joseph, his favorite son. Angry and jealous, Joseph's brothers throw him into a pit and then sell him as a slave. While imprisoned because he spurned the advances of his master's wife, Joseph interprets the dreams of Pharaoh's chief baker and chief butler.

Haftarah (Amos 2:6-3:8): Amos describes the myriad of wrongdoings committed by the Israelites. For their inhumanity to man, they will be punished.

10. *Miketz* (41:1-44:17): Joseph successfully interprets Pharaoh's dreams and is appointed viceroy. His brothers come to Egypt during a famine, seeking food.

Haftarah (I Kings 3:15-4:1): Solomon, Israel's third king, is faced by a complicated situation in which two women both claim the same baby. Solomon decides for the woman who displays the truest motherly love.

11. *Vayigash* (44:18-47:27): Joseph reveals his true identity to his dumbfounded brothers. Then he is reunited with Jacob and the rest of the family.

Haftarah (Ezekiel 37:15-28): Ezekiel promises that the exiled Israelites in Babylon will be reunited in the land of Israel. All who repent will be forgiven by God.

12. *Vayechi* (47:28-50:26): Jacob asks his children to gather together for his final message and blessing. His last request is that his body be brought back to Canaan to be buried in the cave of Machpelah at Hebron.

Haftarah (I Kings 2:1-12): David offers a final blessing to Solomon, his son and successor. David warns Solomon about potential threats to his throne and urges him to remain strong and courageous throughout his life.

Exodus

Contents: The enslavement of the Israelites is described, as well as their eventual emancipation. The book also tells about the Divine Revelation on Mount Sinai and the giving of the Ten Commandments. Numerous religious, civil and moral laws are detailed.

Weekly Portions

1. *Shemot* (1:1-6:1): The infant Moses is saved by Pharaoh's daughter. Later, Moses has a vision of God at the burning bush. God promises to save the Israelites from their enslavement.
Haftarah (Isaiah 27:6-28:13, 29:22-23): Isaiah comforts the Israelites and promises them a better future. He criticizes the citizens of the Northern Kingdom of Israel for their emphasis on material things.

2. *Va-era* (6:2-9:35): Moses and Aaron negotiate with Pharaoh for the freedom of the Israelites. When Pharaoh proves obstinate, God brings a series of plagues upon the Egyptians. Pharaoh remains stubborn and refuses to free the Israelites.
Haftarah (Ezekiel 28:25-29:21): Ezekiel assures the Israelite exiles in Babylon that if they keep faith in God they will return to the Promised Land. He warns those who have remained in Israel not to make a political alliance with Egypt.

3. *Bo* (10:1-13:16): The last three of the ten plagues is described, including the final one, in which all firstborn Egyptian males are slain. On their final night in Egypt, the Israelites celebrate the first Passover. They are commanded to eat roast lamb, matzah and bitter herbs.
Haftarah (Jeremiah 46:13-28): Egypt is defeated by Babylon. The Israelites are consoled and told never to lose hope, for they will one day return to the land of their ancestors.

4. *Beshallach* (13:17-17:16): The Egyptian army is drowned in the Red Sea, but the Israelites are miraculously able to cross. They offer a song of thanksgiving to God.
Haftarah (Judges 4:4-5:31): The prophetess Deborah leads the Israelite army to victory against the Canaanites.

5. *Yitro* (Exodus 18:1-20:23): Moses is reunited with his wife and children. Jethro, his father-in-law, advises him to appoint judges in order to ease his burden. Moses receives the Ten Commandments on Mount Sinai.

Haftarah (Isaiah 6:1-7:6, 9:5-6): Isaiah is reluctant to become a prophet, because he believes he is unworthy of God's trust. Finally convinced that he must assume the responsibility to be God's messenger, he answers, *hineni*, "here I am." Later he urges King Ahaz of Judea to keep his faith and not be afraid of the enemy.

6. *Mishpatim* (Exodus 21:1-24:18): Laws of social justice are put forth on such subjects as slaves, murder, theft, and loans. The portion concludes with the laws concerning the three Pilgrimage Festivals: Sukkot, Passover and Shavuot.

Haftarah (Jeremiah 34:8-22, 33:25-26): Jeremiah condemns King Zedekiah of Judah for failing to free Israelite slaves, warning that God will bring punishment for this wrong. In the future, he says, Israel will be redeemed and will return to the land of its ancestors.

7. *Terumah* (Exodus 25:1-27:19): This deals with the construction of the Tabernacle, Israel's first house of worship. The materials are contributed by the people as free-will offerings.

Haftarah (I Kings 5:26-6:13): King Solomon builds the First Temple.

8. *Tetzaveh* (Exodus 27:20-30:10): The seven-branched menorah (candelabrum) is discussed; it is to be kept burning continuously in front of the Holy of Holies; also vestments of the *kohanim* are described, as are the ancient priests, and the initiating into the assignment of tending to the sanctuary.

Haftarah (Ezekiel 43:10-27): The exiled Israelites must keep their faith in God, for God will one day return them to the Promised Land and the Jerusalem Temple will be rebuilt.

9. *Ki Tissa* (Exodus 30:11-34:35): Instructions are given on taking the census; since every man aged twenty and over is to contribute a half shekel to the sanctuary fund, the number of coins will indicate the number of men eligible for military duty. The golden calf is built, and Moses shows great anger when he sees the idol.

Haftarah (I Kings 18:1-39): This tells of Israel's wrongdoing during the reign of King Ahab. Under the influence of Queen Jezebel, Ahab permits the worship of the god Baal. The prophet Elijah challenges Ahab and Jezebel and persuades the people to proclaim God as the One and only One.

10. *Vayachel* (Exodus 35:1-38:20): Plans are detailed for the building of the Tabernacle.
Haftarah (I Kings 7:40-50): This tells of the artistic work that went into the building of Solomon's Temple.

11. *Pekudei* (38:21-40:38): The building of the Tabernacle is completed; the Israelites are generous in donating materials. On the first anniversary of the exodus from Egypt, the Tabernacle is dedicated.
Haftarah (I Kings 7:51-8:21): The beautiful Temple is built by King Solomon on Mount Zion; there was a joyous dedication during the festival of Sukkot.

Leviticus

Contents: This book deals with the laws that apply to the *kohanim*, the ancient priests. The book details laws pertaining to sacrifices, the Jewish dietary laws, laws of morality, and laws related to the festivals and their observance.

Weekly Portions

1. *Vayikra* (1:1-5:26): The various types of sacrifices brought to the sanctuary are listed; the *kohanim* prepare the sacrifices for burning on the altar.
Haftarah (Isaiah 43:21-44:23): The exiled Israelites in Babylon are warned that believing in idols, mere blocks of carved wood, is foolish. They are told to return to God, Who alone has the power to redeem.

2. *Tzav* (Leviticus 6:1-8:36): The kinds of sacrifices brought to the Tabernacle are described. Aaron and his sons are initiated into their holy assignment as *kohanim*.
Haftarah (Jeremiah 7:21-8:3, 9:22-23): A priest himself, Jeremiah condemns the Israelites for their lack of religiosity and unkindness to others; they will be punished for their behavior.

3. *Shemini* (9:1-11:47): The various kinds of sacrifices are detailed. Nadab and Abihu, Aaron's sons, die after going against the authority of Moses. The beginnings of the laws of keeping kosher are presented.

Haftarah (II Samuel 6:1-7:17): King David brings the Ark of the Covenant to Jerusalem, thus proclaiming the city as Israel's capital. There is dancing and joyous singing in the streets.

4. *Tazri'a* (12:1-13:59): This lists laws of cleanliness and uncleanliness as they relate to childbirth and to leprosy, the most dreaded disease in biblical times.

Haftarah (II Kings 4:42-5:19): The Syrian commander, Naaman, is ill with leprosy, but Elisha cures him using the water from the Jordan River.

5. *Metzora* (14:1-15:33): Various skin diseases are described, with instructions on how they are to be treated by the *kohanim*.

Haftarah (II Kings 7:3-20): Samaria, the capital of the Northern Kingdom, is besieged by Syria. Elisha predicts that God will rescue the city; his prophecy comes true when God causes the Syrians to panic and flee. Four lepers are the first to enter the deserted Syrian camp.

6. *Acharei Mot* (16:1-18:30): This describes in detail the high priest's preparations for Yom Kippur. All Israelites are required to fast and atone on this day.

Haftarah (Ezekiel 22:1-19): The Israelites are warned that they will be punished for their wrongdoings, especially their rejection of family purity and their offering of sacrifices to idols.

7. *Kedoshim* (Leviticus 19:1-20:27): Some important ethical teachings are set forth, including regard for parents, providing for the poor, fair treatment to the stranger, and kindness to the deaf and blind. The law of "love your neighbor as yourself" is presented.

Haftarah (Amos 9:7-15): The Israelites are condemned for their smug confidence. Amos warns that they will be judged and punished for their sins.

8. *Emor* (21:1-24:23): This lists laws of the Sabbath and festivals, duties of the *kohanim*, and the important law of equal treatment for aliens and Israelites.

Haftarah (Ezekiel 44:15-31): The exiled Israelites are assured that they will eventually return to the land of their ancestors. Ezekiel shares a vision of the Jerusalem Temple rebuilt.

9. *Behar* (25:1-26:2): Laws are given related to the Sabbatical Year, when the land was to be rested and slaves set free, and the Jubilee Year, when the land was to lie fallow and be returned to its original owners.

Haftarah (Jeremiah 32:6-27): Jeremiah is thrown in prison. While there, he arranges to purchase land that once belonged to his family, a symbolic act indicating that God will someday permit the Israelites to return to the land of their ancestors.

10. *Bechukotai* (26:3-27:34): Moses warns of the consequences of disobedience. The Israelites will make voluntary contributions for the upkeep of the Tabernacle.

Haftarah (Jeremiah 16:19-17:14): The theme of reward and punishment is reaffirmed. The Israelites ignored Jeremiah's pleas and were punished by Nebuchadnezzar and the Babylonians. But there is hope for the future: redemption is still possible if they return to God and keep the faith.

Numbers

Contents: Most of this book reports on the wanderings of the Israelites in the wilderness en route to the Promised Land.

Weekly Portions

1. *Bemidbar* (1:1-4:20): The census of the Israelites is taken. The Israelites encampment is described. Each tribe has its own special position, with Levi closest to the Tabernacle.

Haftarah (Hosea 2:1-22): The infidelity of Hosea's wife, Gomer, is analogous to the conduct of Israel toward God. Israel will have to pay a penalty for its return to idolatry. In the end, Israel and God will be reunited.

2. *Naso* (4:21-7:89): The Tabernacle duties of the various Levite families are listed, followed by the laws concerning Nazirites, who dedicated themselves to God's service. This portion includes the famous threefold priestly benediction, "May God bless you and keep you."

Haftarah (Judges 13:2-25): Samson is born, and his mother dedicates him as a Nazirite. Because of his Nazirite vow, he is not to cut his hair, drink alcoholic beverages, or have contact with the dead.

3. *Behaalotecha* (8:1-12:16): Aaron lights the seven-branched Menorah and the second Passover is observed. There are several acts of opposition against Moses, including the breaking away of two elders, Eldad and Medad.

Haftarah (Zechariah 2:14-4:7): The prophet offers encouragement and hope to the Israelite returnees from the Babylonian exile. Its most famous line is, "Not by might, nor by power, but by My Spirit, says Adonai Tzeva'ot."

4. *Shelach Lecha* (13:1-15:41): The spies are sent to survey the land of Canaan. Only two of them report that the land can be conquered; they alone of their entire generation are permitted to enter the Promised Land.

Haftarah (Joshua 2:1-24): Joshua sends two spies to Jericho. They are sheltered in the home of Rahab. In return for her help, her life is spared when the city is taken.

5. *Korach* (16:1-18:32): Korach uprises against Moses. He and his followers are punished by being swallowed in an earthquake.

Haftarah (I Samuel 11:14-12:22): God tells Samuel, the last of the judges, to anoint Saul king of Israel.

6. *Chukkat* (Numbers 19:1-22:1): Miriam and Aaron die. God tells Moses to speak to a rock in order to obtain water, but Moses impa-

tiently strikes the rock twice. For this lack of faith, he will not be permitted to enter the Promised Land.

Haftarah (Judges 11:1-33): This Haftarah tells the story of Jephthah, the judge who led the Israelites to victory over Ammon.

7. *Balak* (22:2-25:9): Balak, king of Moab, sends Balaam to curse the Israelites, but Balaam blesses them instead with the words, "How goodly are your tents, O Jacob, your dwelling places, O Israel."

Haftarah (Micah 5:6-6:8): The Assyrians will conquer the Northern Kingdom, but the Israelites will eventually arise again as an example to the nations of the world. The best known verse is: "It has been told, O man, what is good, and what God requires of you. Do justly, love mercy, and walk humbly with your God."

8. *Pinchas* (25:10-30:1): Phinehas, the grandson of Aaron, kills Zimri, a leader of the tribe of Simeon, and is awarded the high priesthood. The daughters of Zelophehad are given their father's inheritance, thus affirming women's rights of inheritance. The daily and festival sacrifices are brought to the Tabernacle.

Haftarah (I Kings 18:46-19:21): Elijah reproves Ahab and Jezebel for worshipping Baal. When the Israelites proclaim their belief in One God, Jezebel becomes angry at Elijah, who flees south. There he is reassured by God that all will be well.

9. *Mattot* (30:2-32:42): The making of vows is discussed. The Israelites are victorious over Midian.

Haftarah (Jeremiah 1:1-2:3): Jeremiah condemns the Israelites for their wrongdoings and urges them to return to God and renew the covenant. God calls to Jeremiah in his youth; Jeremiah is fearful but God reassures him.

10. *Massei* (Numbers 33:1-36:13): The various waystations on the Israelites journey to the Promised Land are listed. Laws pertaining to the six cities of refuge are given.

Haftarah (Jeremiah 2:4-28, 3:4): Jeremiah pleads with the Judeans to stop worshipping idols and return to One God.

Deuteronomy

Contents: The book is a recapitulation of many of the laws previously presented in the Torah, with some additions. Moses delivers several farewell addresses to the Israelites in which he reviews the wanderings of the people and repeats the Ten Commandments. Moses dies at the end of the book.

Weekly Portions

1. *Devarim* (1:1-3:22): Moses gives his first address: the Israelites journey from Sinai to the Promised Land; Israel defeats the Amorites and King Og of Bashan.
Haftarah (Isaiah 1:1-17): Isaiah condemns the Judeans. The bringing of sacrifices is not enough; God wants justice and righteousness.

2. *Va'etchanan*(3:23-7:11): Moses gives his second address, including a review of the Ten Commandments.
Haftarah (Isaiah 40:1-26): The Babylonian exiles are assured that God has forgiven them and that better times lie ahead of their return to the Promised Land.

3. *Ekev* (7:12-11:25): Moses' farewell address continues, asking the people to remember the past and never take God for granted. The second paragraph of the *Shema* prayer appears in this portion, dealing with the theme of reward and punishment.
Haftarah (Isaiah 49:14-51:3): This is a comforting message for the exiled Israelites. God will restore them and return them to the Holy Land.

4. *Re'eh* (11:26-16:17): Moses continues his farewell address, reminding the Israelites that obedience to God will bring blessing, while disobedience will only bring curses. The laws of the tithe and the Sabbatical Year are described.
Haftarah (Isaiah 54:11-55:5): The exiled Israelites are asked to keep their faith in God, Who will return them to Zion.

5. *Shofetim* (16:18-21-9): Moses warns against idolatry. The monarch is discussed; the functions of the king, as well as the limitations of his power, are described.
Haftarah (Isaiah 51:12-52:12): A message of hope is offered to the exiles in Babylonia; Jerusalem will soon be redeemed and they will rejoice again in the land of their ancestors.

6. *Ki-tetze* (21:10-25:19): Various laws are detailed intended to strengthen family life and human decency, including lost property, educational responsibilities of parents, and kindness to animals.
Haftarah (Isaiah 54:1-10): Isaiah gives a message of confidence to the Babylonian exiles. There will be a renewed covenant of peace between God and Israel.

7. *Ki Tavo* (26:1-29:8): The laws of tithing and first fruits are detailed. Moses' third address begins here; the Israelites are to erect twelve stones on Mount Ebal and inscribe the laws on them.
Haftarah (Isaiah 60:1-22): The Babylonian exiles are assured that they will be restored as a community in the Promised Land.

8. *Nitzavim* (29:9-30:20): Moses' third address continues, explaining that God's covenant was given not only to the generation of the exodus but to all future generations.
Haftarah (Isaiah 61:10-63:9): The exiled Israelites are told to prepare for their return to the Holy Land.

9. *Vayelech* (31:1-30): Moses appoints Joshua as his successor. He assures the Israelites that they have no need to be afraid, for God will be with them and will guide Joshua as he guided Moses.
Haftarah (Hosea 16:2-20, Micah 7:18-20, Joel 2:15-27): This Haftarah, consisting of selections from three prophets, is the one assigned for the Sabbath of Repentance, which occurs between Rosh Hashanah and Yom Kippur. The theme is repentance and returning to God, Who will forgive those who truly and sincerely repent.

10. *Ha'azinu* (32:1-52): This is Moses' farewell song, written as a poem. Moses calls upon heaven and earth to witness God's depend-

ability and urges all nations to join with Israel in its great song of deliverance.

Haftarah (II Samuel 22:1-51): In a song of thanksgiving, King David expresses gratitude to God for his deliverance from the enemy. The final verse, describing God as a tower of salvation, is also the concluding verse of the Grace after Meals.

11. *Vezot Haberacha* (33:1-34:12): In Moses' final address, he blesses the tribes of Israel, and shortly thereafter he dies on Mount Nebo.

Haftarah (Joshua 1:1-18): Joshua's career begins. The Israelites cross the Jordan River into the Promised Land. The strategy for the conquest of Canaan is outlined.

Haftarot for Special Sabbaths and Selected Festivals

1. Rosh Hodesh, Sabbath coinciding with New Moon (Isaiah 66:1-24): The faithful Israelites are contrasted with the nonbelievers who follow after idols. One God will be worshipped universally: "It shall come to pass from one new moon to another, and from one Sabbath to another, all flesh shall come to worship Me" (v. 23).

2. Machar Hodesh, eve of the New Moon (I Samuel 20:18-42): The story of the friendship between Jonathan and David is told. This Haftarah is read on the eve of a new Jewish month because it begins with "Tomorrow is the new moon."

3. Sukkot, first day (Zechariah 14:1-21): Zechariah presents a powerful vision of God's judgment upon the enemy nations. Israel will be redeemed from their hands.

4. Sukkot, second day (I Kings 8:2-21): The First Temple is dedicated by King Solomon. The festivities extended over fourteen days, of which the last seven days were the days of Sukkot.

5. Sukkot, Intermediate Sabbath (Ezekiel 38:18-39:16): The restoration of Israel to its land is prophesied. According to tradition,

the war of final victory described by Ezekiel will be waged during the festival of Sukkot.

6. Shemini Atzeret (I Kings 8:54-66): First Temple is dedicated by King Solomon. The last seven days of the dedication took place during Sukkot.

7. Hanukkah, first Sabbath (Zechariah 2:14-4:7): The Israelites are urged to "sing and rejoice," for God will be with them again. The vision of the menorah at the conclusion is the link to Hanukkah.

8. Hanukkah, second Sabbath (I Kings 7:40-50): The objects used in the First Temple are described. This Haftarah is read during Hanukkah because it was at that time, after the defeat of Antiochus, that the Temple was rededicated (*Hanukkah* literally means "dedication").

9. Shabbat Shekalim (II Kings 12:1-17): Athaliah, the daughter of Ahab and Jezebel, promoted Baal worship in Judah. The people revolted and removed her from the throne. She was succeeded by her grandson Jehoash, who cleansed the Temple. This Haftarah is read on the Sabbath of Shekalim, when we are reminded of the half shekel given to maintain the ancient Tabernacle, because Jehoash told the *kohanim* to collect money for Temple repairs. The Haftarah is read on the Sabbath immediately preceding the month of Adar.

10. Shabbat Zachor (I Samuel 15:1-34): This Haftarah tells of Amalek's aggression against Israel. It is read on the Sabbath preceding Purim because Haman, who tried to destroy the Persian Jews, was a descendant of Amalek.

11. Shabbat Parah (Ezekiel 36:16-38): A message of comfort is offered to the exiled Israelites. If they purify themselves morally, God will forgive them and restore them to their homeland. The theme of purity helps to set the mood for the forthcoming Passover festival.

12. Shabbat HaHodesh (Ezekiel 45:16-46:18): This Haftarah sets the tone for Passover by discussing the Passover sacrifices. It is read on the Sabbath before the beginning of Nisan, when Passover occurs.

13. Shabbat HaGadol (Malachi 3:4-24): When Israel attains true and authentic spirituality, the complete redemption of Israel and humankind will follow. This is read on the Sabbath before Passover because Passover is the festival of redemption.

14. Shavuot, first day (Ezekiel 1:1-28, 3:12): Ezekiel sees a vision of the Divine Throne-Chariot and four-faced living creatures, suggesting that God moves everywhere and thus will be with the Israelites during their exile in Babylon.

15. Shavuot, second day (Habakkuk 2:20-23): The prophet pleads with God to intervene on behalf of the Israelites. In a vision he sees God coming from afar, disguised as a warrior. God will redeem Israel from persecution.

Glossary

Aliyah (plural *aliyot*). Lit. "going up"; the ascent to the bimah to say the Torah blessings.
Aufruf. Custom of calling groom to the Torah for an aliyah on the Sabbath prior to his wedding.
Bar. Aramaic for "son."
Bat. Hebrew for "daughter."
Birkat Hamazon. Blessing after the meal.
Chumash. The Five Books of Moses.
Derashah. Explanation of Torah reading, sometimes called a *devar torah.*
Gelilah. Honor of "dressing" the Torah after it has been lifted.
Haftarah. Selection from prophetic or historical books of Bible, read following Torah reading.
Hagbah. Honor of lifting the Torah scroll.
Hamotzi. Blessing over bread.
Kiddush. Blessing over wine. Also refers to refreshments served after Saturday morning service.
Kohen (plural *kohanim).* Descendant of priestly family.
Midrash. Rabbinic interpretation of biblical verse.
Mitzvah (plural *mitzvot.*) Religious commandment.
Pentateuch. Five Books of Moses.
Petichah (plural *petichot).* Honor of opening the Holy Ark.
Rosh Hodesh. Celebration of a new Jewish month.
Seudat Mitzvah. Festive meal following the Jewish rite of passage, such as Bar or Bat Mitzvah.
Shehecheyanu. Prayer for the gift of life.
Simchah. Joyous occasion.
Torah. First part of the Hebrew Bible; it consists of Genesis, Exodus, Leviticus, Numbers and Deuteronomy. Also known as Five Books of Moses and as Pentateuch.
Tzedakah. Lit. "righteousness"; the mitzvah of righteous giving.

Torah. First part of the Hebrew Bible; it consists of Genesis, Exodus, Leviticus, Numbers and Deuteronomy. Also known as Five Books of Moses and as Pentateuch.

Tzedakah. Lit. "righteousness"; the mitzvah of righteous giving.